CONVENTION
BETWEEN
THE GOVERNMENT OF THE UNITED STATES OF AMERICA
AND
THE GOVERNMENT OF THE KINGDOM OF DENMARK
FOR THE AVOIDANCE OF DOUBLE TAXATION
AND THE PREVENTION OF FISCAL EVASION
WITH RESPECT TO TAXES ON INCOME

The Government of the United States of America and the Government of the Kingdom

of Denmark, desiring to conclude a Convention for the avoidance of double taxation and the

prevention of fiscal evasion with respect to taxes on income, have agreed as follows:

ARTICLE 1

General Scope

1. Except as otherwise provided in this Convention, this Convention shall apply to persons who are residents of one or both of the Contracting States.

2. This Convention shall not restrict in any manner any benefit now or hereafter accorded:

a) by the laws of either Contracting State; or

b) by any other agreement between the Contracting States.

3. Notwithstanding the provisions of subparagraph 2 b):

a) the provisions of Article 25 (Mutual Agreement Procedure) of this Convention exclusively shall apply to any dispute concerning whether a measure is within the scope of this Convention, and the procedures under this Convention exclusively shall apply to that dispute; and

b) unless the competent authorities determine that a taxation measure is not within the scope of this Convention, the non-discrimination obligations of this Convention exclusively shall apply with respect to that measure, except for such national treatment or most-favored-nation obligations as may apply to trade in goods under the General Agreement on Tariffs and Trade. No national treatment or most-favored-nation obligation under any other agreement shall apply with respect to that measure.

c) For the purpose of this paragraph, a "measure" is a law, regulation, rule, procedure, decision, administrative action, or any similar provision or action.

4. Notwithstanding any provision of the Convention except paragraph 5 of this Article, a Contracting State may tax its residents (as determined under Article 4 (Residence)), and by reason of citizenship may tax its citizens, as if the Convention had not come into effect. For this purpose, the term "citizen" shall include a former citizen or long-term resident whose loss of such status had as one of its principal purposes the avoidance of tax (as defined under the laws of the Contracting State of which the person was a citizen or long-term resident), but only for a period of 10 years following such loss.

5. The provisions of paragraph 4 shall not affect:

a) the benefits conferred by a Contracting State under paragraph 2 of Article 9 (Associated Enterprises), paragraphs 7 and 8 of Article 13 (Capital Gains), paragraphs 1 c), 2 and 5 of Article 18 (Pensions, Social Security, Annuities, Alimony and Child Support Payments), and Articles 23 (Relief from Double Taxation), 24 (Non-Discrimination), and 25 (Mutual Agreement Procedure); and

b) the benefits conferred by a Contracting State under Articles 19 (Government Service), 20 (Students and Trainees) and 28 (Diplomatic Agents and Consular Officers), upon individuals who are neither citizens of, nor have been admitted for permanent residence in, that State.

ARTICLE 2

Taxes Covered

1. The existing taxes to which this Convention applies are:

a) in the United States:

(i) the Federal income taxes imposed by the Internal Revenue Code (but excluding social security taxes); and

(ii) the Federal excise taxes imposed with respect to private foundations;

b) in Denmark:

(i) the income tax to the State (indkomstskatten til staten);

(ii) the municipal income tax (den kommunale indkomstskat);

(iii) the income tax to the county municipalities (den amtskommunale indkomstskat); and

(iv) taxes imposed under the Hydrocarbon Tax Act (skatter i henhold til kulbrinteskatteloven).

2. The Convention shall apply also to any identical or substantially similar taxes which are imposed after the date of signature of the Convention in addition to, or in place of, the

existing taxes. The competent authorities of the Contracting States shall notify each other of any significant changes that have been made in their respective taxation laws or other laws affecting their obligations under the Convention, and of any official published material concerning the application of this Convention, including explanations, regulations, rulings, or judicial decisions.

ARTICLE 3

General Definitions

1. For the purposes of this Convention, unless the context otherwise requires:

a) the term "person" includes an individual, an estate, a trust, a partnership, a company and any other body of persons;

b) the term "company" means any body corporate or any entity which is treated as a body corporate for tax purposes according to the laws of the state in which it is organized;

c) the terms "enterprise of a Contracting State" and "enterprise of the other Contracting State" mean respectively an enterprise carried on by a resident of a Contracting State, and an enterprise carried on by a resident of the other Contracting State; the terms also include an enterprise carried on by a resident of a Contracting State through an entity that is treated as fiscally transparent in that Contracting State;

d) the term "international traffic" means any transport by a ship or aircraft, except when such transport is solely between places in a Contracting State;

e) the term "competent authority" means:

(i) in the United States: the Secretary of the Treasury or his delegate; and

(ii) in Denmark: the Minister for Taxation or his authorized representative;

f) the term "United States" means the United States of America, and includes the states thereof and the District of Columbia; such term also includes the territorial sea thereof and the sea bed and subsoil of the submarine areas adjacent to that territorial sea, over which the United States exercises sovereign rights in accordance with international law; the term, however, does not include Puerto Rico, the Virgin Islands, Guam or any other United States possession or territory.

g) the term "Denmark" means the Kingdom of Denmark, including any area outside the territorial sea of Denmark which in accordance with international law has been or may hereafter be designated under Danish laws as an area within which Denmark may exercise sovereign rights with respect to the exploration and exploitation of the natural resources of the sea-bed or its subsoil and the superjacent waters and with respect to other activities for the exploration and economic exploitation of the area; the term "Denmark" does not comprise the Faroe Islands or Greenland;

h) the term "national of a Contracting State," means:

(i) any individual possessing the nationality or citizenship of that State; and

(ii) any legal person, partnership or association deriving its status as such from the laws in force in that State;

i) the term "qualified governmental entity" means:

(i) any person or body of persons that constitutes a governing body of a Contracting State, or of a political subdivision or local authority of a Contracting State;

(ii) a person that is wholly owned, directly or indirectly, by a Contracting State or political subdivision or local authority of a Contracting State, provided it is organized under the laws of the Contracting State, its earnings are credited to its own account with no portion of its income inuring to the benefit of any private person, and its assets vest in the Contracting State, political subdivision or local authority upon dissolution; and

(iii) a pension trust or fund of a person described in clause (i) or (ii) that is constituted and operated exclusively to administer or provide pension benefits described in Article 19 (Government Service);

provided that an entity described in clause (ii) or (iii) does not carry on commercial activities.

2. As regards the application of the Convention at any time by a Contracting State any term not defined therein shall, unless the context otherwise requires, or the competent authorities agree to a common meaning pursuant to the provisions of Article 25 (Mutual Agreement Procedure), have the meaning which it has at that time under the law of that State for the purposes of the taxes to which the Convention applies, any meaning under the applicable tax laws of that State prevailing over a meaning given to the term under other laws of that State.

ARTICLE 4

Residence

1. Except as provided in this paragraph, for the purposes of this Convention, the term "resident of a Contracting State" means any person who, under the laws of that State, is liable to tax therein by reason of his domicile, residence, citizenship, place of management, place of incorporation, or any other criterion of a similar nature.

a) The term "resident of a Contracting State" does not include any person who is liable to tax in that State in respect only of income from sources in that State or of profits attributable to a permanent establishment in that State.

b) A legal person organized under the laws of a Contracting State and that is generally exempt from tax in that State and is established and maintained in that State either:

(i) exclusively for a religious, charitable, educational, scientific, or other similar purpose; or

(ii) to provide pensions or other similar benefits to employees, including self-employed individuals, pursuant to a plan

is to be treated for purposes of this paragraph as a resident of that Contracting State.

c) A qualified governmental entity is to be treated as a resident of the Contracting State where it is established.

d) An item of income, profit or gain derived through an entity that is fiscally transparent under the laws of either Contracting State shall be considered to be derived by a resident of a State to the extent that the item is treated for purposes of the taxation law of such Contracting State as the income, profit or gain of a resident.

2. Where by reason of the provisions of paragraph 1 an individual is a resident of both Contracting States, then his status shall be determined as follows:

a) the individual shall be deemed to be a resident of the State in which he has a permanent home available to him; if such individual has a permanent home available to him in both States, he shall be deemed to be a resident of the State with which his personal and economic relations are closer (center of vital interests);

b) if the State in which the individual has his center of vital interests cannot be determined, or if he has no permanent home available to him in either State, he shall be deemed to be a resident of the State in which he has an habitual abode;

c) if the individual has an habitual abode in both States or in neither of them, he shall be deemed to be a resident of the State of which he is a national;

d) if he is a national of both States or of neither of them, the competent authorities of the Contracting States shall endeavor to settle the question by mutual agreement.

3. Where by reason of the provisions of paragraph 1 a person other than an individual is a resident of both Contracting States, the competent authorities of the Contracting States shall by mutual agreement endeavor to settle the question and to determine the mode of application of the Convention to such person.

4. A United States citizen or an alien lawfully admitted for permanent residence in the United States is a resident of the United States, but only if such person has a substantial presence, permanent home or habitual abode in the United States.

ARTICLE 5

Permanent Establishment

1. For the purposes of this Convention, the term "permanent establishment" means a fixed place of business through which the business of an enterprise is wholly or partly carried on.

2. The term "permanent establishment" includes especially:

    a) a place of management;

    b) a branch;

    c) an office;

    d) a factory;

    e) a workshop; and

    f) a mine, an oil or gas well, a quarry, or any other place of extraction of natural resources.

3. A building site or construction or installation project, or an installation or drilling rig or ship used for the exploration of natural resources, constitutes a permanent establishment only if it lasts, or the activity continues for, more than 12 months. For the purpose of this paragraph, activities carried on by an enterprise related to another enterprise, within the meaning of Article 9 (Associated Enterprises), shall be regarded as carried on by the enterprise to which it is related if the activities in question:

    a) are substantially the same as those carried on by the last-mentioned enterprise; and

    b) are concerned with the same project or operation;

except to the extent that those activities are carried on at the same time.

4. Notwithstanding the preceding provisions of this Article, the term "permanent establishment" shall be deemed not to include:

    a) the use of facilities solely for the purpose of storage, display, or delivery of goods or merchandise belonging to the enterprise;

    b) the maintenance of a stock of goods or merchandise belonging to the enterprise solely for the purpose of storage, display, or delivery;

c) the maintenance of a stock of goods or merchandise belonging to the enterprise solely for the purpose of processing by another enterprise;

d) the maintenance of a fixed place of business solely for the purpose of purchasing goods or merchandise, or of collecting information, for the enterprise;

e) the maintenance of a fixed place of business solely for the purpose of carrying on, for the enterprise, any other activity of a preparatory or auxiliary character;

f) the maintenance of a fixed place of business solely for any combination of the activities mentioned in subparagraphs a) to e) of this paragraph, provided that the overall activity of the fixed place of business resulting from the combination is of a preparatory or auxiliary character.

5. Notwithstanding the provisions of paragraphs 1 and 2, where a person -- other than an agent of an independent status to whom paragraph 6 applies -- is acting on behalf of an enterprise and has and habitually exercises in a Contracting State an authority to conclude contracts in the name of the enterprise, that enterprise shall be deemed to have a permanent establishment in that State in respect of any activities which that person undertakes for the enterprise, unless the activities of such person are limited to those mentioned in paragraph 4 which, if exercised through a fixed place of business, would not make this fixed place of business a permanent establishment under the provisions of that paragraph.

6. An enterprise shall not be deemed to have a permanent establishment in a Contracting State merely because it carries on business in that State through a broker, general commission agent, or any other agent of an independent status, provided that such persons are acting in the ordinary course of their business as independent agents.

7. The fact that a company that is a resident of a Contracting State controls or is controlled by a company that is a resident of the other Contracting State, or which carries on business in that other State (whether through a permanent establishment or otherwise), shall not constitute either company a permanent establishment of the other.

ARTICLE 6

Income from Real Property

1. Income derived by a resident of a Contracting State from real property (including income from agriculture or forestry) situated in the other Contracting State may be taxed in that other State.

2. The term "real property" shall have the meaning which it has under the law of the Contracting State in which the property in question is situated. The term shall in any case include property accessory to real property, livestock and equipment used in agriculture and forestry, rights to which the provisions of general law respecting landed property apply, usufruct of real property, and rights to variable or fixed payments as consideration for the working of, or the right to work, mineral deposits, sources and other natural resources; ships, boats and aircraft shall not be regarded as real property.

3. The provisions of paragraph 1 shall apply to income derived from the direct use, letting, or use in any other form of real property.

4. The provisions of paragraphs 1 and 3 shall also apply to the income from real property of an enterprise and to income from real property used for the performance of independent personal services.

5. A resident of a Contracting State who is liable to tax in the other Contracting State on income from real property situated in the other Contracting State may elect for any taxable year to compute the tax on such income on a net basis as if such income were business profits attributable to a permanent establishment in such other State. Any such election shall be binding for the taxable year of the election and all subsequent taxable years unless the competent authority of the Contracting State in which the property is situated agrees to terminate the election.

ARTICLE 7

Business Profits

1. The business profits of an enterprise of a Contracting State shall be taxable only in that State unless the enterprise carries on business in the other Contracting State through a permanent establishment situated therein. If the enterprise carries on business as aforesaid, the business profits of the enterprise may be taxed in the other State but only so much of them as is attributable to that permanent establishment.

2. Subject to the provisions of paragraph 3, where an enterprise of a Contracting State carries on business in the other Contracting State through a permanent establishment situated therein, there shall in each Contracting State be attributed to that permanent establishment the business profits which it might be expected to make if it were a distinct and independent enterprise engaged in the same or similar activities under the same or similar conditions. For this purpose, the business profits to be attributed to the permanent establishment shall include only the profits derived from the assets or activities of the permanent establishment.

3. In determining the business profits of a permanent establishment, there shall be allowed as deductions expenses which are incurred for the purposes of the permanent establishment, including a reasonable allocation of executive and general administrative expenses, research and development expenses, interest, and other expenses incurred for the purposes of the enterprise as a whole (or the part thereof which includes the permanent establishment), whether incurred in the State in which the permanent establishment is situated or elsewhere.

4. No business profits shall be attributed to a permanent establishment by reason of the mere purchase by that permanent establishment of goods or merchandise for the enterprise.

5. For the purposes of the preceding paragraphs, the profits to be attributed to the permanent establishment shall be determined by the same method year by year unless there is good and sufficient reason to the contrary.

6. Where business profits include items of income which are dealt with separately in other Articles of this Convention, then the provisions of those Articles shall not be affected by

the provisions of this Article.

7. For the purposes of this Convention, the term "business profits" means income from any trade or business, including income derived by an enterprise from the performance of personal services, and from the rental of tangible personal property.

8. In applying paragraphs 1 and 2 of Article 7 (Business Profits), paragraph 6 of Article 10 (Dividends), paragraph 3 of Article 11 (Interest), paragraph 3 of Article 12 (Royalties), paragraph 3 of Article 13 (Capital Gains), Article 14 (Independent Personal Services), and paragraph 2 of Article 21 (Other Income), any income or gain attributable to a permanent establishment or fixed base during its existence is taxable in the Contracting State where such permanent establishment or fixed base is situated even if the payments are deferred until such permanent establishment or fixed base has ceased to exist.

ARTICLE 8

Shipping and Air Transport

1. Profits of an enterprise of a Contracting State from the operation in international traffic of ships or aircraft shall be taxable only in that State.

2. For the purposes of this Article, profits from the operation of ships or aircraft include profits derived from the rental of ships or aircraft on a full (time or voyage) basis. They also include profits from the rental of ships or aircraft on a bareboat basis if such ships or aircraft are operated in international traffic by the lessee, or if the rental income is incidental to profits from the operation of ships or aircraft in international traffic. Profits derived by an enterprise from the inland transport of property or passengers within either Contracting State, shall be treated as profits from the operation of ships or aircraft in international traffic if such transport is undertaken as part of international traffic.

3. Profits of an enterprise of a Contracting State from the use, maintenance or rental of containers (including trailers, barges, and related equipment for the transport of containers) used in international traffic shall be taxable only in that State.

4. The provisions of paragraphs 1 and 3 shall also apply to profits from the participation

in a consortium, a pool, a joint business, or an international operating agency.

5. Notwithstanding the provisions of subparagraph 2 f) and paragraph 3 of Article 5 (Permanent Establishment), the profits of an enterprise of a Contracting State from the transport by ships or aircraft of supplies or personnel to a location where offshore activities in connection with the exploration or exploitation of natural resources are being carried on in the other Contracting State, or from the operation of tugboats and similar vessels in connection with such activities, shall be taxable only in the first-mentioned State.

ARTICLE 9

Associated Enterprises

1. Where

a) an enterprise of a Contracting State participates, directly or indirectly, in the management, control, or capital of an enterprise of the other Contracting State, or

b) the same persons participate directly or indirectly in the management, control, or capital of an enterprise of a Contracting State and an enterprise of the other Contracting State,

and in either case conditions are made or imposed between the two enterprises in their commercial or financial relations which differ from those which would be made between independent enterprises, then any profits which, but for those conditions, would have accrued to one of the enterprises, but by reason of those conditions, have not so accrued, may be included in the profits of that enterprise and taxed accordingly.

2. Where a Contracting State includes in the profits of an enterprise of that State, and taxes accordingly, profits on which an enterprise of the other Contracting State has been charged to tax in that other State, and the other Contracting State agrees that the profits so included are profits that would have accrued to the enterprise of the first-mentioned State if the conditions made between the two enterprises had been those which would have been made between independent enterprises, then that other State shall make an appropriate adjustment to the amount of the tax charged therein on those profits. In determining such adjustment, due

regard shall be had to the other provisions of this Convention and the competent authorities of the Contracting States shall if necessary consult each other.

ARTICLE 10

Dividends

1. Dividends paid by a resident of a Contracting State to a resident of the other Contracting State may be taxed in that other State.

2. However, such dividends may also be taxed in the Contracting State of which the company paying the dividends is a resident and according to the laws of that State, but if the beneficial owner of the dividends is a resident of the other Contracting State the tax so charged shall not exceed:

a) 5 percent of the gross amount of the dividends if the beneficial owner is a company which holds directly at least 10 percent of the share capital of the company paying the dividends;

b) 15 percent of the gross amount of the dividends in all other cases.

This paragraph shall not affect the taxation of the company in respect of the profits out of which the dividends are paid.

3. Subparagraph a) of paragraph 2 shall not apply in the case of dividends paid by a United States Regulated Investment Company (RIC) or United States Real Estate Investment Trust (REIT). In the case of dividends from a RIC, subparagraph b) of paragraph 2 shall apply. In the case of dividends paid by a REIT, subparagraph b) of paragraph 2 shall apply only if:

a) the beneficial owner of the dividends is an individual holding an interest of not more than 10 percent in the REIT;

b) the dividends are paid with respect to a class of stock that is publicly traded and the beneficial owner of the dividends is a person holding an interest of not more than 5 percent of any class of the REIT's stock; or

c) the beneficial owner of the dividends is a person holding an interest of not more than 10 percent in the REIT and the REIT is diversified.

4. Notwithstanding paragraph 2, dividends may not be taxed in the Contracting State of which the payor is a resident if the beneficial owner of the dividends is a resident of the other Contracting State that is a qualified governmental entity that does not control the payor of the dividend.

5. The term "dividends" as used in this Article means income from shares or other rights, not being debt-claims, participating in profits, as well as income that is subject to the same taxation treatment as income from shares by the laws of the State of which the payor is a resident.

6. The provisions of paragraphs 1 and 2 shall not apply if the beneficial owner of the dividends, being a resident of a Contracting State, carries on business in the other Contracting State of which the payor is a resident, through a permanent establishment situated therein, or performs in that other State independent personal services from a fixed base situated therein, and the dividends are attributable to such permanent establishment or fixed base. In such case, the provisions of Article 7 (Business Profits) or Article 14 (Independent Personal Services), as the case may be, shall apply.

7. A Contracting State may not impose any tax on dividends paid by a resident of the other State, except insofar as the dividends are paid to a resident of the first-mentioned State or the dividends are attributable to a permanent establishment or a fixed base situated in that State, nor may it impose tax on a corporation's undistributed profits, except as provided in paragraph 8, even if the dividends paid or the undistributed profits consist wholly or partly of profits or income arising in that State.

8. A corporation that is a resident of one of the States and that has a permanent establishment in the other State or that is subject to tax in the other State on a net basis on its income that may be taxed in the other State under Article 6 (Income from Real Property) or under paragraph 1 of Article 13 (Capital Gains) may be subject in that other State to a tax in addition to the tax allowable under the other provisions of this Convention. Such tax, however, may be imposed on only the portion of the business profits of the corporation attributable to the permanent establishment and the portion of the income referred to in the preceding sentence that

is subject to tax under Article 6 (Income from Real Property) or under paragraph 1 of Article 13

(Capital Gains) that, in the case of the United States, represents the dividend equivalent amount

of such profits or income and, in the case of Denmark, is an amount that is analogous to the

dividend equivalent amount.

9. The tax referred to in paragraph 8 may not be imposed at a rate in excess of the rate

specified in subparagraph a) of paragraph 2.

ARTICLE 11

Interest

1. Interest arising in a Contracting State and beneficially owned by a resident of the other

Contracting State shall be taxable only in that other State.

2. The term "interest" as used in this Article means income from debt-claims of every

kind, whether or not secured by mortgage, and whether or not carrying a right to participate in

the debtor's profits, and in particular, income from government securities and income from

bonds or debentures, including premiums or prizes attaching to such securities, bonds, or

debentures, and all other income that is subjected to the same taxation treatment as income from

money lent by the taxation law of the Contracting State in which the income arises. Income

dealt with in Article 10 (Dividends) and penalty charges for late payment shall not be regarded

as interest for the purposes of this Article.

3. The provisions of paragraph 1 shall not apply if the beneficial owner of the interest,

being a resident of a Contracting State, carries on business in the other Contracting State in

which the interest arises, through a permanent establishment situated therein, or performs in that

other State independent personal services from a fixed base situated therein, and the interest is

attributable to such permanent establishment or fixed base. In such case the provisions of

Article 7 (Business Profits) or Article 14 (Independent Personal Services), as the case may be,

shall apply.

4. Where, by reason of a special relationship between the payor and the beneficial owner

or between both of them and some other person, the amount of the interest, having regard to the debt-claim for which it is paid, exceeds the amount which would have been agreed upon by the payor and the beneficial owner in the absence of such relationship, the provisions of this Article shall apply only to the last-mentioned amount. In such case, the excess part of the payments shall remain taxable according to the laws of each State, due regard being had to the other provisions of this Convention.

5. Notwithstanding the provisions of paragraph 1:

a) interest paid by a resident of a Contracting State and that is determined with reference to receipts, sales, income, profits or other cash flow of the debtor or a related person, to any change in the value of any property of the debtor or a related person or to any dividend, partnership distribution or similar payment made by the debtor to a related person, and paid to a resident of the other State also may be taxed in the Contracting State in which it arises, and according to the laws of that State, but if the beneficial owner is a resident of the other Contracting State, the gross amount of the interest may be taxed at a rate not exceeding the rate prescribed in subparagraph b) of paragraph 2 of Article 10 (Dividends); and

b) interest that is an excess inclusion with respect to a residual interest in a real estate mortgage investment conduit may be taxed by each State in accordance with its domestic law.

ARTICLE 12

Royalties

1. Royalties arising in a Contracting State and beneficially owned by a resident of the other Contracting State shall be taxable only in that other State.

2. The term "royalties" as used in this Article means:

a) any consideration for the use of, or the right to use, any copyright of literary, artistic, scientific or other work (including computer software, cinematographic films, audio or video tapes or disks, and other means of image or sound reproduction), any patent, trademark, design or model, plan, secret formula or process, or other like right or property, or for information concerning industrial, commercial or scientific experience; and

      b) gain derived from the alienation of any property described in subparagraph a), provided that such gain is contingent on the productivity, use or disposition of the property.

3. The provisions of paragraph 1 shall not apply if the beneficial owner of the royalties, being a resident of a Contracting State, carries on business in the other Contracting State in which the royalties arise, through a permanent establishment situated therein, or performs in that other State independent personal services from a fixed base situated therein, and the royalties are attributable to such permanent establishment or fixed base. In such case the provisions of Article 7 (Business Profits) or Article 14 (Independent Personal Services), as the case may be, shall apply.

4. Where, by reason of a special relationship between the payor and the beneficial owner or between both of them and some other person, the amount of the royalties, having regard to the use, right, or information for which they are paid, exceeds the amount which would have been agreed upon by the payor and the beneficial owner in the absence of such relationship, the provisions of this Article shall apply only to the last-mentioned amount. In such case, the excess part of the payments shall remain taxable according to the laws of each Contracting State, due regard being had to the other provisions of this Convention.

ARTICLE 13

Capital Gains

1. Gains derived by a resident of a Contracting State that are attributable to the alienation of real property situated in the other Contracting State may be taxed in that other State.

2. For the purposes of this Article, the term "real property situated in the other Contracting State" shall include:

      a) real property referred to in Article 6 (Income from Real Property);

b) a United States real property interest; and

c) an equivalent interest in real property situated in Denmark.

3. Gains from the alienation of personal property that are attributable to a permanent establishment that an enterprise of a Contracting State has in the other Contracting State or that are attributable to a fixed base that is available to a resident of a Contracting State in the other Contracting State for the purpose of performing independent personal services, and gains from the alienation of such a permanent establishment (alone or with the whole enterprise) or of such a fixed base, may be taxed in that other State.

4. Notwithstanding the provisions of paragraph 3, gains derived by an enterprise of a Contracting State from the alienation of ships, boats, aircraft, or containers operated or used in international traffic or personal property pertaining to the operation or use of such ships, boats, aircraft, or containers shall be taxable only in that State.

5. Gains derived by an enterprise of a Contracting State from the deemed alienation of an installation, drilling rig, or ship used in the other Contracting State for the exploration for or exploitation of oil and gas resources may be taxed in that other State in accordance with its law, but only to the extent of any depreciation taken in that other State.

6. Gains from the alienation of any property, other than that referred to in paragraphs 1 through 5, shall be taxable only in the Contracting State of which the alienator is a resident.

7. If a resident of a Contracting State is subject to income taxation in both Contracting States on a disposition of property and is treated as having alienated property with respect to which a gain is recognized under the income tax laws of the other Contracting State, then the resident not otherwise required to do so may elect in his annual return of income for the year of the alienation to be liable to tax in the residence State in that year as if he had, immediately before that time, sold and repurchased such property for an amount equal to its fair market value at that time. Such an election shall apply to all property described in this paragraph that is alienated by the resident in the taxable year for which the election is made or at any time thereafter.

8. Where a resident of a Contracting State alienates property in the course of a

corporate or other organization, reorganization, amalgamation, division or similar transaction and profit, gain or income with respect to such alienation is not recognized for the purpose of taxation in that State, the competent authority of the other Contracting State may agree, if requested to do so by the person who acquires the property, in order to avoid double taxation and subject to terms and conditions satisfactory to such competent authority, to defer the recognition of the profit, gain or income with respect to such property for the purpose of taxation in that other State until such time and in such manner as may be stipulated in the agreement.

ARTICLE 14

Independent Personal Services

1. Income derived by an individual who is a resident of a Contracting State in respect of the performance of personal services of an independent character shall be taxable only in that State, unless the individual has a fixed base regularly available to him in the other Contracting State for the purpose of performing his activities. If he has such a fixed base, the income attributable to the fixed base that is derived in respect of services performed in that other State also may be taxed by that other State.

2. For purposes of paragraph 1, the income that is taxable in the other Contracting State shall be determined under the principles of paragraph 3 of Article 7 (Business Profits).

ARTICLE 15

Dependent Personal Services

1. Subject to the provisions of Articles 16 (Directors' Fees), 18 (Pensions, Social Security, Annuities, Alimony and Child Support Payments), and 19 (Government Service), salaries, wages and other remuneration derived by a resident of a Contracting State in respect of an employment shall be taxable only in that State unless the employment is exercised in the other Contracting State. If the employment is so exercised, such remuneration as is derived therefrom may be taxed in that other State.

2. Notwithstanding the provisions of paragraph 1, remuneration derived by a resident of a Contracting State in respect of an employment exercised in the other Contracting State shall be taxable only in the first-mentioned State if:

a) the recipient is present in the other State for a period or periods not exceeding in the aggregate 183 days in any twelve month period commencing or ending in the taxable year concerned; and

b) the remuneration is paid by, or on behalf of, an employer who is not a resident of the other State; and

c) the remuneration is not borne by a permanent establishment or a fixed base which the employer has in the other State.

3. Notwithstanding the preceding provisions of this Article, remuneration described in paragraph 1 that is derived by a resident of a Contracting State in respect of an employment as a member of the regular complement of a ship or aircraft operated in international traffic shall be taxable only in that State.

ARTICLE 16

Directors' Fees

Directors' fees and other similar payments derived by a resident of a Contracting State in his capacity as a member of the board of directors of a company which is a resident of the other Contracting State may be taxed in that other State.

ARTICLE 17

Artistes and Sportsmen

1. Income derived by a resident of a Contracting State as an entertainer, such as a theater, motion picture, radio, or television artiste, or a musician, or as a sportsman, from his personal activities as such exercised in the other Contracting State, which income would be exempt from tax in that other Contracting State under the provisions of Articles 14 (Independent Personal Services) and 15 (Dependent Personal Services), may be taxed in that

other State, except where the amount of the gross receipts derived by such entertainer or sportsman, including expenses reimbursed to him, or borne on his behalf, from such activities does not exceed twenty thousand United States dollars ($20,000) or its equivalent in Danish kroner for the taxable year concerned.

2. Where income in respect of activities exercised by an entertainer or a sportsman in his capacity as such accrues not to the entertainer or sportsman himself but to another person, that income may, notwithstanding the provisions of Articles 7 (Business Profits) and 14 (Independent Personal Services), be taxed in the Contracting State in which the activities of the entertainer or sportsman are exercised, unless the entertainer or sportsman establishes that neither the entertainer or sportsman nor persons related thereto participate directly or indirectly in the profits of that other person in any manner, including the receipt of deferred remuneration, bonuses, fees, dividends, partnership distributions, or other distributions.

ARTICLE 18

Pensions, Social Security, Annuities, Alimony

and Child Support Payments

1. Subject to the provisions of paragraph 2 of Article 19 (Government Service),

a) Except as provided in subparagraph b), pension distributions arising in a Contracting State and beneficially owned by a resident of the other Contracting State shall be taxable only in the State in which they arise;

b) If, prior to the time of entry into force of this Convention, a person was a resident of a Contracting State and was receiving pension distributions arising in the other Contracting State, that person shall be taxable on pension distributions referred to in subparagraph a) only in the first-mentioned Contracting State;

c) Pension distributions shall be deemed to arise in a Contracting State only if paid by a pension scheme established in that State.

d) For purposes of this paragraph, pension distributions means pension distributions and other similar remuneration, whether paid periodically or as a single sum.

2. Notwithstanding the provisions of paragraph 1, payments made by a Contracting State under provisions of the social security or similar legislation of that Contracting State to a resident of the other Contracting State or to a citizen of the United States shall be taxable only in the first-mentioned State.

3. Annuities derived and beneficially owned by an individual resident of a Contracting State shall be taxable only in that State. The term "annuities" as used in this paragraph means a stated sum paid periodically at stated times during a specified number of years or for life under an obligation to make the payments in return for adequate and full consideration (other than services rendered).

4. Alimony paid by a resident of a Contracting State, and deductible therein, to a resident of the other Contracting State shall be taxable only in that other Contracting State. The term "alimony" as used in this paragraph means periodic payments made pursuant to a written separation agreement or a decree of divorce, separate maintenance, or compulsory support, which payments are taxable to the recipient under the laws of the State of which he is a resident.

5. Periodic payments, not dealt with in paragraph 4, for the support of a child made pursuant to a written separation agreement or a decree of divorce, separate maintenance, or compulsory support, paid by a resident of a Contracting State to a resident of the other Contracting State, shall be taxable only in the first-mentioned Contracting State.

ARTICLE 19

Government Service

1. Notwithstanding the provisions of Articles 14 (Independent Personal Services), 15 (Dependent Personal Services), 16 (Directors' Fees) and 17 (Artistes and Sportsmen):

a) Salaries, wages and other remuneration, other than a pension, paid from the public funds of a Contracting State or a political subdivision or a local authority thereof to an individual in respect of services rendered to that State or subdivision or authority in the discharge of functions of a governmental nature shall, subject to the provisions of subparagraph b), be taxable only in that State;

b) such remuneration, however, shall be taxable only in the other Contracting State if the services are rendered in that State and the individual is a resident of that State who:

(i) is a national of that State; or

(ii) did not become a resident of that State solely for the purpose of rendering the services.

2. a) Any pension paid from the public funds of a Contracting State or a political subdivision or a local authority thereof to an individual in respect of services rendered to that State or subdivision or authority in the discharge of functions of a governmental nature (other than a payment described in paragraph 2 of Article 18 (Pensions, Social Security, Annuities, Alimony and Child Support Payments)) shall, subject to the provisions of subparagraph b), be taxable only in that State;

b) such pension, however, shall be taxable only in the other Contracting State if the individual is a resident or a national of that State.

3. The provisions of Articles 15 (Dependent Personal Services), 16 (Directors' Fees), 17 (Artistes and Sportsmen) and 18 (Pensions, Social Security, Annuities, Alimony and Child Support Payments) shall apply to remuneration and pensions in respect of services rendered in connection with a business carried on by a Contracting State or a political subdivision or a local authority thereof.

ARTICLE 20

Students and Trainees

Payments received by a student, apprentice, or business trainee who is, or was immediately before visiting a Contracting State, a resident of the other Contracting State, and who is present in the first-mentioned State for the purpose of his full-time education at an accredited educational institution, or for his full-time training, shall not be taxed in that State, provided that such payments arise outside that State, and are for the purpose of his maintenance, education or training. The exemption from tax provided by this Article shall apply to an apprentice or business trainee only for a period of time not exceeding three years from the date he first arrives in the first-mentioned Contracting State for the purpose of his training. The provisions of this paragraph shall not apply to income from research if such research is undertaken not in the public interest but primarily for the private benefit of a specific person or persons.

ARTICLE 21

Other Income

1. Items of income beneficially owned by a resident of a Contracting State, wherever arising, not dealt with in the foregoing Articles of this Convention shall be taxable only in that State.

2. The provisions of paragraph 1 shall not apply to income, other than income from real property as defined in paragraph 2 of Article 6 (Income from Real Property), if the beneficial owner of such income, being a resident of a Contracting State, carries on business in the other Contracting State through a permanent establishment situated therein, or performs in the other State independent personal services from a fixed base situated therein, and the income is attributable to such permanent establishment or fixed base. In such case the provisions of Article 7 (Business Profits) or Article 14 (Independent Personal Services), as the case may be, shall apply.

ARTICLE 22

Limitation of Benefits

1. A resident of a Contracting State shall be entitled to the benefits of this Convention only to the extent provided in this Article.

2. A resident of a Contracting State shall be entitled to all the benefits of this Convention only if such resident is:

    a) an individual;

    b) a Contracting State, a political subdivision, or local authority thereof, or an agency or instrumentality of that State, subdivision, or authority;

c) a company if:

(i) all the shares in the class or classes of shares representing more than 50 percent of the vote and value are listed on a recognized stock exchange and are substantially and regularly traded on one or more recognized stock exchanges;

(ii) one or more taxable nonstock corporations entitled to benefits under paragraph g) own shares representing more than 50 percent of the voting power of the company and all other shares are listed on a recognized stock exchange and are substantially and regularly traded on one or more recognized stock exchanges; or

(iii) at least 50 percent of each class of shares in the company is owned, directly or indirectly, by five or fewer companies entitled to benefits under clause (i) or (ii), or any combination thereof, provided that in the case of indirect ownership, each intermediate owner is a person entitled to benefits of the Convention under this paragraph;

d) a charitable organization or other legal person described in subparagraph b)(i) of paragraph 1 of Article 4 (Residence);

e) a legal person, whether or not exempt from tax, organized under the laws of a Contracting State to provide a pension or other similar benefits to employees, including self-employed individuals, pursuant to a plan, provided that more than 50 percent of the person's beneficiaries, members or participants are individuals resident in either Contracting State; or

f) a person, other than an individual, if

(i) on at least half the days of the taxable year, persons described in subparagraphs a), b), c), d), or e) own, directly or indirectly (through a chain of ownership in which each person is entitled to the benefits of the Convention under this paragraph), at least 50 percent of the beneficial interest in such person (or, in the case of a company, at least 50 percent of the vote and value of the company's shares); and

(ii) less than 50 percent of the person's gross income for the taxable year is paid or accrued, in the form of deductible payments, directly or indirectly, to persons who are not residents of either Contracting State (unless the payment is attributable to a permanent establishment situated in either State);

g) in the case of Denmark, a taxable nonstock corporation if

(i) the amount paid or accrued in the form of deductible payments in the taxable year and in each of the preceding three taxable years, directly or indirectly, to persons who are not entitled to benefits under subparagraphs a), b), c)(i), c)(iii) by virtue of c)(i), d) or e), does not exceed 50% of the amount of its gross income (excluding its tax-exempt income); and

(ii) the amount paid or accrued, in the form of both deductible payments and non-deductible distributions, in the taxable year and in each of the preceding three taxable years, directly or indirectly, to persons who are not entitled to benefits under subparagraphs a), b), c)(i), c(iii) by virtue of c(i), d), or e), does not exceed 50% of the amount of its total income (including its tax-exempt income).

3.   a) A resident of a Contracting State not otherwise entitled to benefits shall be entitled to the benefits of this Convention with respect to an item of income derived from the other Contracting State if:

(i) the resident is engaged in the active conduct of a trade or business in the first-mentioned Contracting State;

(ii) the income is connected with or incidental to the trade or business in the first-mentioned Contracting State; and

(iii) the trade or business is substantial in relation to the activity in the other State generating the income.

b) For purposes of this paragraph, the business of making or managing investments will not be considered an active trade or business, unless the activity is banking, insurance or securities activities carried on by a bank, insurance company, or registered securities dealer.

c) Whether a trade or business is substantial for purposes of this paragraph will be determined based on all the facts and circumstances. In any case, however, a trade or business will be deemed substantial if, for the preceding taxable year, or for the average of the three preceding taxable years, the asset value, the gross income, and the payroll expense that are related to the trade or business in the first-mentioned State equal at least 7.5 percent of the resident's (and any related parties') proportionate share of the asset value, gross income and payroll expense, respectively, that are related to the activity that generated the income in the other State, and the average of the three ratios exceeds 10 percent. In determining the above ratios, assets, income, and payroll expense shall be taken into account only to the extent of the resident's direct or indirect ownership interest in the activity in the other State. If neither the resident nor any of its associated enterprises has an ownership interest in the activity in the other State, the resident's trade or business in the first-mentioned State shall be considered substantial in relation to such activity.

d) Income is derived in connection with a trade or business if the activity in the other State generating the income is a line of business that forms part of or is complementary to the trade or business. Income is incidental to a trade or business if it facilitates the conduct of the trade or business in the other State.

4.   a) A company that is a resident of a Contracting State shall also be entitled to all of the benefits of the Convention if:

> (i) at least 95 percent of the aggregate vote and value of all its shares is owned, directly or indirectly, by seven or fewer persons that are residents of Member States of the European Union, or of the European Economic Area, or of parties to the North American Free Trade Agreement (NAFTA) that, in any

case, meet the requirements of subparagraph c), or any combination thereof;
and

(ii) less than 50 percent of the company's gross income for the
taxable year is paid or accrued, in the form of deductible payments, directly or
indirectly, to persons who are not residents of Member States of the European
Union, or of the European Economic Area, or of parties to the North American
Free Trade Agreement that, in any case, meet the requirements of subparagraph
c), or any combination thereof.

b) However, a company otherwise entitled to benefits under subparagraph a)
will not be entitled to the benefits of this Convention if that company, or a company that
controls such company, has outstanding a class of shares:

(i) the terms of which, or which is subject to other arrangements
that, entitle its holders to a portion of the income of the company derived from
the other Contracting State that is larger than the portion such holders would
receive absent such terms or arrangements; and

(ii) 50 percent or more of the vote or value of which is owned by
persons who are not residents of a Member State of the European Union or the
European Economic Area or a party to the North American Free Trade
Agreement that, in any case, meet the requirements of subparagraph c), or any
combination thereof.

c) For purposes of subparagraphs a) and b), a person will be treated as a
resident of a Member State of the European Union or of the European Economic Area
or of a party to the North American Free Trade Agreement only if such person:

(i) would be entitled to the benefits of a comprehensive income tax
convention in force between any Member State of the European Union or of
the European Economic Area or a party to the North American Free Trade
Agreement and the Contracting State from which the benefits of this
Convention are claimed, provided that if such other convention does not

contain a comprehensive limitation on benefits article (including provisions similar to those of subparagraphs c) and f) of paragraph 2 and paragraph 3 of this Article), the person would be entitled to the benefits of this Convention under the principles of paragraph 2 if such person were a resident of one of the Contracting States under Article 4 (Residence) of this Convention; and

(ii) with respect to income referred to in Articles 10 (Dividends), 11 (Interest) or 12 (Royalties), would be entitled under such other convention to a rate of tax with respect to the particular class of income for which benefits are being claimed under this Convention that is at least as low as the rate applicable under this Convention.

5. A resident of one of the Contracting States that derives from the other Contracting State income mentioned in Article 8 (Shipping and Air Transport) and that is not entitled to the benefits of this Convention because of the foregoing paragraphs, shall nevertheless be entitled to the benefits of this Convention with respect to such income if at least 50% of the beneficial interest in such person (or in the case of a company, at least 50% of the aggregate vote and value of the stock of such company) is owned directly or indirectly:

a) by persons described in subparagraphs a), b), c), d), or e) of paragraph 2, or citizens of the United States, or individuals who are residents of a third state; or

b) by a company or combination of companies the stock of which is primarily and regularly traded on an established securities market in a third state, provided that such third state grants an exemption under similar terms for profits as mentioned in Article 8 (Shipping and Air Transport) of this Convention to citizens and corporations of the other Contracting State either under its national law or in common agreement with that other Contracting State or under a convention between that third state and the other Contracting State.

6. The following rules and definitions shall apply for purposes of this Article:

a) in measuring "gross income", as used in subparagraph f) of paragraph 2, the term means gross income for the first taxable period preceding the current taxable period, provided that the amount of gross income for the first taxable period preceding the current taxable period shall be deemed to be no less than the average of the annual amounts of gross income for the four taxable periods preceding the current taxable period;

      b) the term "deductible payments"

          (i) as used in subparagraphs f) and g) of paragraph 2 and subparagraph a) of paragraph 4 includes payments for interest or royalties, but does not include payments at arm's length for the purchase or use of or the right to use tangible property in the ordinary course of business or remuneration at arm's length for services performed in the Contracting State in which the person making such payments is a resident; and

          (ii) as used in subparagraph g) of paragraph 2 also includes deductible distributions made by a taxable nonstock corporation.

Types of payments may be added to, or eliminated from, the exceptions mentioned in the preceding definition of "deductible payments" by mutual agreement of the competent authorities;

      c) For the purposes of this Article, the term "recognized stock exchange" means:

          (i) the NASDAQ System owned by the National Association of Securities Dealers, Inc. and any stock exchange registered with the U.S. Securities and Exchange Commission as a national securities exchange for purposes of the U.S. Securities Exchange Act of 1934;

          (ii) the Copenhagen Stock Exchange and the stock exchanges of Amsterdam, Brussels, Frankfurt, Hamburg, London, Paris, Stockholm, Sydney, Tokyo and Toronto;

          (iii) any other stock exchanges agreed upon by the competent authorities of both Contracting States;

      d) the term "engaged in the active conduct of a trade or business" in a

Contracting State as used in paragraph 3, applies to a person that is directly so engaged, or is a partner in a partnership that is so engaged, or is so engaged through one or more associated enterprises (wherever resident);

e) the term "taxable nonstock corporation" as used in paragraph 2 means a foundation that is taxable in accordance with paragraph 1 of Article 1 of the Danish Act on Taxable Nonstock Corporations (fonde der beskattes efter fondsbeskatningsloven).

f) (i) For the purposes of paragraph 2, the shares in a class of shares are considered to be substantially and regularly traded on one or more recognized stock exchanges in a taxable year if:

(1) trades in such class are effected on one or more of such stock exchanges other than in de minimis quantities during every quarter; and

(2) the aggregate number of shares or units of that class traded on such stock exchange or exchanges during the previous taxable year is at least 6 percent of the average number of shares or units outstanding in that class (including shares held by taxable nonstock corporations) during that taxable year.

(ii) For purposes of determining whether a company satisfies the requirements of clause (c)(ii) of paragraph 2, clause (i) of this subparagraph shall be applied as if all the shares issued by the company were one class of shares, and shares held by taxable nonstock corporations will be considered outstanding for purposes of determining whether 6 percent of the outstanding shares have been traded during a taxable year.

7. A resident of a Contracting State that is not entitled to the benefits of the Convention under the provisions of the preceding paragraphs of this Article shall, nevertheless, be granted the benefits of the Convention if the competent authority of the other Contracting State so determines.

ARTICLE 23

Relief from Double Taxation

1. In accordance with the provisions and subject to the limitations of the law of the United States (as it may be amended from time to time without changing the general principle hereof), the United States shall allow to a resident or citizen of the United States as a credit against the United States tax on income:

a) the income tax paid or accrued to Denmark by or on behalf of such resident or citizen; and

b) in the case of a United States company owning at least 10 percent of the voting stock of a company that is a resident of Denmark and from which the United States company receives dividends, the income tax paid or accrued to Denmark by or on behalf of the payor with respect to the profits out of which the dividends are paid.

c) (i) Subject to the provisions of clause (ii), in the case of a resident or national of the United States subject to the taxes imposed by the Hydrocarbon Tax Act that are referred to in subparagraph b)(iv) of paragraph 1 of Article 2 (Taxes Covered), the United States shall allow as a credit against the United States tax on income, the appropriate amount of tax paid or accrued to Denmark by or on behalf of such resident or national pursuant to the Hydrocarbon Tax Act on oil and gas extraction income from oil or gas wells in Denmark. However, the appropriate amount allowed as a credit shall not exceed the product of the maximum statutory United States tax rate applicable to such resident or national for such taxable year, and the amount of income separately assessed under the Hydrocarbon Tax Act.

(ii) The appropriate amount is also subject to any other limitations imposed by the law of the United States, as it may be amended from time to time, that apply to creditable taxes under section 901 or 903 of the Internal Revenue Code for persons claiming benefits under this Convention. Any taxes paid on income assessed separately under the Hydrocarbon Tax Act in excess of the appropriate amount may be used only as a credit in another taxable year, and only against United States tax on income assessed separately under the Hydrocarbon Tax Act.

(iii) The provisions of clauses (i) and (ii) shall apply separately, in the same way, to the amount of tax paid or accrued to Denmark pursuant to the Hydrocarbon Tax Act on (1) Danish source oil related income not described in clause (i); and (2) other Danish source income.

For the purposes of this Article, the Danish taxes referred to in paragraphs 1(b) and 2 of Article 2 (Taxes Covered) shall be considered income taxes and shall be allowed as a credit against the United States tax on income, subject to all the provisions and limitations of this paragraph.

2. Where a United States citizen is a resident of Denmark:

a) with respect to items of income that under the provisions of this Convention are exempt from United States tax or that are subject to a reduced rate of United States tax when derived by a resident of Denmark who is not a United States citizen, Denmark shall allow as a credit against Danish tax only the tax paid, if any, that the United States may impose under the provisions of this Convention, other than taxes that may be imposed solely by reason of citizenship under the saving clause of paragraph 4 of Article 1 (General Scope);

b) for purposes of computing United States tax on those items of income referred to in subparagraph a), the United States shall allow as a credit against United States tax the income tax paid to Denmark after the credit referred to in subparagraph a); the credit so allowed shall not reduce the portion of the United States tax that is creditable against the Danish tax in accordance with subparagraph a); and

c) for the exclusive purpose of relieving double taxation in the United States under subparagraph b), items of income referred to in subparagraph a) shall be deemed to arise in Denmark to the extent necessary to avoid double taxation of such income under subparagraph b).

3. In the case of Denmark, double taxation shall be avoided as follows:

a) When a resident of Denmark derives income which, in accordance with the provisions of this Convention, may be taxed in the United States, Denmark shall allow as a deduction from the tax on the income of that resident an amount equal to the income tax paid in the United States;

b) Such deduction shall not, however, exceed that part of the income tax, as computed before the deduction is given, which is attributable to the income that may be taxed in the United States.

c) When a resident of Denmark derives income which, in accordance with the provisions of this Convention, shall be taxable only in the United States, Denmark may include this income in the tax base but shall allow as a deduction from income tax that part of the income tax which is attributable to the income derived from the United States.

For the purposes of this paragraph, the United States taxes referred to in paragraphs 1(a) and 2 of Article 2 (Taxes Covered) shall be considered income taxes, and shall be allowed as a credit against the Danish tax on income.

ARTICLE 24

Non-Discrimination

1. Nationals of a Contracting State shall not be subjected in the other Contracting State to any taxation or any requirement connected therewith that is more burdensome than the taxation and connected requirements to which citizens of that other State in the same circumstances, particularly with respect to taxation of worldwide income, are or may be subjected. This provision shall also apply to persons who are not residents of one or both of the Contracting States.

2. The taxation on a permanent establishment or fixed base that a resident or enterprise of a Contracting State has in the other Contracting State shall not be less favorably levied in that other State than the taxation levied on enterprises or residents of that other State carrying on the same activities. The provisions of this paragraph shall not be construed as obliging a

Contracting State to grant to residents of the other Contracting State any personal allowances, reliefs, and reductions for taxation purposes on account of civil status or family responsibilities which it grants to its own residents.

3. Except where the provisions of paragraph 1 of Article 9 (Associated Enterprises), paragraph 4 of Article 11 (Interest), or paragraph 4 of Article 12 (Royalties) apply, interest, royalties and other disbursements paid by an enterprise of a Contracting State to a resident of the other Contracting State shall, for the purpose of determining the taxable profits of such enterprise, be deductible under the same conditions as if they had been paid to a resident of the first-mentioned State. Similarly, any debts of an enterprise of a Contracting State to a resident of the other Contracting State shall, for the purpose of determining the taxable capital of the first-mentioned resident, be deductible under the same conditions as if they had been contracted to a resident of the first-mentioned State.

4. Enterprises of a Contracting State, the capital of which is wholly or partly owned or controlled, directly or indirectly, by one or more residents of the other Contracting State, shall not be subjected in the first-mentioned State to any taxation or any requirement connected therewith that is more burdensome than the taxation and connected requirements to which other similar enterprises of the first-mentioned State are or may be subjected.

5. Nothing in this Article shall be construed as preventing either Contracting State from imposing a tax as described in paragraph 8 of Article 10 (Dividends).

6. The provisions of this Article shall, notwithstanding the provisions of Article 2 (Taxes Covered), apply to taxes of every kind and description imposed by a Contracting State or a political subdivision or local authority thereof.

ARTICLE 25

Mutual Agreement Procedure

1. Where a person considers that the actions of one or both of the Contracting States result or will result for him in taxation not in accordance with the provisions of this Convention, he may, irrespective of the remedies provided by the domestic law of those States and the time

limits prescribed in such laws for presentation of claims for refund, present his case to the competent authority of the Contracting State of which he is a resident or national.

2. The competent authority shall endeavour, if the objection appears to it to be justified and if it is not itself able to arrive at a satisfactory solution, to resolve the case by mutual agreement with the competent authority of the other Contracting State, with a view to the avoidance of taxation which is not in accordance with the Convention. Any agreement reached shall be implemented notwithstanding any time limits in the domestic law of the Contracting States. Assessment and collection procedures shall be suspended during the pendency of any mutual agreement proceeding.

3. The competent authorities of the Contracting States shall endeavour to resolve by mutual agreement any difficulties or doubts arising as to the interpretation or application of the Convention. In particular the competent authorities of the Contracting States may agree:

a) to the same attribution of income, deductions, credits, or allowances of an enterprise of a Contracting State to its permanent establishment situated in the other Contracting State;

b) to the same allocation of income, deductions, credits, or allowances between persons;

c) to the same characterization of particular items of income, including the same characterization of income that is assimilated to income from shares by the taxation law of one of the Contracting States and that is treated as a different class of income in the other State;

d) to the same characterization of persons;

e) to the same application of source rules with respect to particular items of income;

f) to a common meaning of a term;

g) to advance pricing arrangements; and

h) to the application of the provisions of domestic law regarding penalties, fines, and interest in a manner consistent with the purposes of the Convention.

They may also consult together for the elimination of double taxation in cases not provided for in the Convention.

4. The competent authorities also may agree to increases in any specific dollar amounts referred to in the Convention to reflect economic or monetary developments.

5. The competent authorities of the Contracting States may communicate with each other directly for the purpose of reaching an agreement in the sense of the preceding paragraphs.

ARTICLE 26

Exchange of Information

1. The competent authorities of the Contracting States shall exchange such information as is relevant for carrying out the provisions of this Convention or of the domestic laws of the Contracting States concerning taxes covered by the Convention insofar as the taxation thereunder is not contrary to the Convention, including information relating to the assessment or collection of, the enforcement or prosecution in respect of, or the determination of appeals in relation to, the taxes covered by the Convention. The exchange of information is not restricted by Article 1 (General Scope). Any information received by a Contracting State shall be treated as secret in the same manner as information obtained under the domestic laws of that State and shall be disclosed only to persons or authorities (including courts and administrative bodies) involved in the assessment, collection, or administration of, the enforcement or prosecution in respect of, or the determination of appeals in relation to, the taxes covered by the Convention or the oversight of the above. Such persons or authorities shall use the information only for such purposes. They may disclose the information in public court proceedings or in judicial decisions.

2. In no case shall the provisions of paragraph 1 be construed so as to impose on a Contracting State the obligation:

a) to carry out administrative measures at variance with the laws and administrative practice of that or of the other Contracting State;

b) to supply information which is not obtainable under the laws or in the normal course of the administration of that or of the other Contracting State; or

c) to supply information which would disclose any trade, business, industrial, commercial, or professional secret or trade process, or information the disclosure of which would be contrary to public policy (ordre public).

3. Notwithstanding paragraph 2, the competent authority of the requested State shall have the authority to obtain and provide information held by financial institutions, nominees or persons acting in an agency or fiduciary capacity, or respecting interests in a person. If information is requested by a Contracting State in accordance with this Article, the other Contracting State shall obtain that information in the same manner and to the same extent as if the tax of the first-mentioned State were the tax of that other State and were being imposed by that other State, notwithstanding that the other State may not, at that time, need such information for purposes of its own tax. If specifically requested by the competent authority of a Contracting State, the competent authority of the other Contracting State shall provide information under this Article in the form of depositions of witnesses and authenticated copies of unedited original documents (including books, papers, statements, records, accounts, and writings), to the same extent such depositions and documents can be obtained under the laws and administrative practices of that other State with respect to its own taxes.

4. For purposes of this Article, the Convention shall apply, notwithstanding the provisions of Article 2 (Taxes Covered), to taxes of every kind imposed by a Contracting State.

ARTICLE 27

Administrative Assistance

1. The Contracting States undertake to lend assistance to each other in the collection of taxes referred to in Article 2 (Taxes Covered), together with interest, costs, additions to such taxes, and civil penalties, referred to in this Article as a "revenue claim."

2. An application for assistance in the collection of a revenue claim shall include a certification by the competent authority of the applicant State that, under the laws of that State, the revenue claim has been finally determined. For the purposes of this Article, a revenue claim is finally determined when the applicant State has the right under its internal law to collect the

revenue claim and all administrative and judicial rights of the taxpayer to restrain collection in the applicant State have lapsed or been exhausted.

3. A revenue claim of the applicant State that has been finally determined may be accepted for collection by the competent authority of the requested State and, subject to the provisions of paragraph 7, if accepted shall be collected by the requested State as though such revenue claim were the requested State's own revenue claim finally determined in accordance with the laws applicable to the collection of the requested State's own taxes.

4. Where an application for collection of a revenue claim in respect of a taxpayer is accepted

> a) by the United States, the revenue claim shall be treated by the United States as an assessment under United States laws against the taxpayer as of the time the application is received; and

> b) by Denmark, the revenue claim shall be treated by Denmark as an assessment under Danish laws against the taxpayer as of the time the application is received.

5. Nothing in this Article shall be construed as creating or providing any rights of administrative or judicial review of the applicant State's finally determined revenue claim by the requested State, based on any such rights that may be available under the laws of either Contracting State. If, at any time pending execution of a request for assistance under this Article, the applicant State loses the right under its internal law to collect the revenue claim, the competent authority of the applicant State shall promptly withdraw the request for assistance in collection.

6. Subject to this paragraph, amounts collected by the requested State pursuant to this Article shall be forwarded to the competent authority of the applicant State. Unless the competent authorities of the Contracting States otherwise agree, the ordinary costs incurred in providing collection assistance shall be borne by the requested State and any extraordinary costs so incurred shall be borne by the applicant State.

7. A revenue claim of an applicant State accepted for collection shall not have in the

requested State any priority accorded to the revenue claims of the requested State.

8. No assistance shall be provided under this Article for a revenue claim in respect of a taxpayer to the extent that the taxpayer can demonstrate that

a) where the taxpayer is an individual, the revenue claim relates to a taxable period in which the taxpayer was a citizen of the requested State, and

b) where the taxpayer is an entity that is a company, estate or trust, the revenue claim relates to a taxable period in which the taxpayer derived its status as such an entity from the laws in force in the requested State.

9. Each of the Contracting States shall endeavor to collect on behalf of the other Contracting State such amounts as may be necessary to ensure that relief granted by the Convention from taxation imposed by that other State does not inure to the benefit of persons not entitled thereto.

10. Nothing in this Article shall be construed as imposing on either Contracting State the obligation to carry out administrative measures of a different nature from those used in the collection of its own taxes or that would be contrary to its public policy (ordre public).

11. The competent authorities of the Contracting States shall agree upon the mode of application of this Article, including agreement to ensure comparable levels of assistance to each of the Contracting States.

12. The requested State shall not be obliged to accede to the request of the applicant State:

a) if the applicant State has not pursued all appropriate collection action in its own jurisdiction; or

b) in those cases where the administrative burden for the requested State is disproportionate to the benefit to be derived by the applicant State.

ARTICLE 28

Diplomatic Agents and Consular Officers

Nothing in this Convention shall affect the fiscal privileges of diplomatic agents or consular officers under the general rules of international law or under the provisions of special agreements.

ARTICLE 29

Entry into Force

1. The Contracting States shall notify each other when the requirements for the entry into force of this Convention have been complied with.

2. The Convention shall enter into force on the date of the receipt of the later of such notifications, and its provisions shall have effect:

a) in respect of taxes withheld at source, for amounts paid or credited on or after the first day of the second month next following the date on which the Convention enters into force;

b) in respect of other taxes, for taxable periods beginning on or after the first day of January next following the date on which the Convention enters into force.

3. Subject to paragraph 4, the Convention between Denmark and the United States for the Avoidance of Double Taxation and the Prevention of Fiscal Evasion with Respect to Taxes on Income signed at Washington, D.C., on May 6, 1948 (hereinafter referred to as "the 1948 Convention") shall cease to have effect when the provisions of this Convention take effect in accordance with paragraph 2 or 4.

4. Where the 1948 Convention would have afforded any person any greater relief from tax than this Convention, the 1948 Convention shall, at the election of any person that was entitled to benefits under the prior Convention, continue to have effect in its entirety for one year after the date on which the provisions of this Convention would otherwise first have effect pursuant to paragraph 2.

5. The 1948 Convention shall terminate on the last date on which it has effect in

accordance with the foregoing provisions of this Article.

ARTICLE 30

Termination

This Convention shall remain in force until terminated by a Contracting State. Either Contracting State may terminate the Convention by giving notice of termination through diplomatic channels. In such event, the Convention shall cease to have effect:

a) in respect of taxes withheld at source, for amounts paid or credited after the expiration of the 6-month period beginning on the date on which notice of termination was given; and

b) in respect of other taxes, for taxable periods beginning on or after the expiration of the 6-month period beginning on the date on which notice of termination was given.

IN WITNESS WHEREOF, the undersigned, being duly authorized by their respective

Governments, have signed this Convention.

DONE at Washington in the English language, this ___ day of _____, 1999.

FOR THE GOVERNMENT OF THE   FOR THE GOVERNMENT OF THE
UNITED STATES OF AMERICA: KINGDOM OF DENMARK:

PROTOCOL

At the signing today of the Convention between the Government of the United States of America and the Government of the Kingdom of Denmark for the Avoidance of Double Taxation and the Prevention of Fiscal Evasion with Respect to Taxes on Income ("the Convention"), the undersigned have agreed on the following provisions, which shall form an integral part of the Convention.

1. Scandinavian Airlines System (SAS) is a consortium within the meaning of Article 8 (Shipping and Air Transport), its participating members being SAS Danmark A/S, SAS Norge ASA and SAS Sverige AB. In order to avoid the problems inherent in operating in the United States through a consortium, the members of the consortium in 1946 established a New York corporation, Scandinavian Airlines System, Inc. (SAS, Inc.) to act on their behalf in the United States pursuant to an agency agreement dated September 18, 1946. A similar agreement was entered into by SAS directly and SAS, Inc., on March 14, 1951. Pursuant to the agency agreement, SAS, Inc., is authorized to perform only such functions as SAS assigns to it, all in connection with international air traffic. Under that agreement, all revenues collected by SAS, Inc., are automatically credited to SAS. Operation expenses incurred by SAS, Inc., are debited to SAS in accordance with the terms of the agency agreement. SAS is obligated under the terms of the agency agreement to reimburse SAS, Inc. for all of its expenses irrespective of the revenues of SAS, Inc. SAS, Inc., does not perform any functions except those connected with or incidental to the business of SAS as an operator of aircraft in international traffic.

In view of the special nature of the SAS consortium and in view of the agency agreement as described above, the United States for purposes of Article 8 (Shipping and Air Transport) of the Convention shall treat all of the income earned by SAS, Inc., that is derived from the operation in international traffic of aircraft as the income of the SAS consortium.

2. This Convention may be extended either in its entirety or with any necessary modifications to any part of Denmark to which the Convention does not apply and which imposes taxes substantially similar in character to those to which the Convention applies. Such extension shall take effect from such date, shall be subject to such modification and conditions as may be specified in a supplementary Convention agreed between the Contracting States, and

shall enter into force in accordance with their constitutional procedures.

3. Articles 7 (Business Profits) and 24 (Non-Discrimination) shall not prevent Denmark from continuing to tax permanent establishments of United States insurance companies in accordance with section 12, paragraph 3, of the Danish Company Tax law nor shall it prevent the United States from continuing to tax permanent establishments of Danish insurance companies in accordance with section 842(b) of the Internal Revenue Code.

4.   a) A payment shall be treated as a pension distribution under paragraph 1 of Article 18 (Pensions, Social Security, Annuities, Alimony and Child Support Payments) if it is a payment under a pension scheme recognized for tax purposes in the Contracting State where the pension scheme is established.

b) For this purpose, pension schemes recognized for tax purposes shall include the following and any identical or substantially similar schemes which are imposed after the date of signature of the Convention:

(i) Under United States law, qualified plans under section 401(a) of the Internal Revenue Code, individual retirement plans (including individual retirement plans that are part of a simplified employee pension plan that satisfies section 408(k), individual retirement accounts, individual retirement annuities, section 408(p) accounts, and Roth IRAs under section 408A), section 403(a) qualified annuity plans, and section 403(b) plans.

(ii) Under the law of Denmark, pension schemes under Section I of the Act on Taxation of Pension Schemes (pensionsbeskatningslovens afsnit I).

3

IN WITNESS WHEREOF, the undersigned, being duly authorized by their respective

Governments, have signed this Protocol.

DONE at Washington in the English language, this ___ day of _____, 1999.

FOR THE GOVERNMENT OF THE
UNITED STATES OF AMERICA:

FOR THE GOVERNMENT OF THE
KINGDOM OF DENMARK:

www.ingramcontent.com/pod-product-compliance
Lightning Source LLC
Chambersburg PA
CBHW060651290526
45793CB00001B/497